Copyright Daniel Arnold 2018.

Lansing Riverfront Press

The Super Hero Life

By Daniel K. Arnold

Other Books By Daniel K. Arnold

The Super Hero Manual

The Super Hero Manual Trilogy

Ever Changing

Black Bird Ops

Journalists For Jesus

Obey God.

To Be A Man

Culmination Of A Miracle

#Satisfied

The Super Hero Structure

Talk to God

The Super Hero Life

Table of Contents

#Satisfied

by

Daniel K. Arnold

Preface:

What can I create and do with the resources God has given me now? I love writing in a new notebook and impacting people.

I want you to know that you matter—to God and to me.

Let's enjoy this journey to meaning and purpose of life together.

<u>Chapter 1 – Slow</u>

It is important to slow down and go for quality, not quantity. Most books were not written in a day; the same is to be said for our story.

Take it easy and find the silver lining no matter what your situation.

Thanks be to God!

Thanks be to God for the good and the bad. Thanks be to God for shaping me in the fire of hard circumstances.

Thanks be to God for giving me life.

Thanks for the little things. When I was suicidal in the hospital, I wanted to punch the wall. I was livid and frustrated.

Next, God rolled out the red carpet. The nurse kindly asked me if I wanted a hot blanket.

At that moment, I had to take the focus off of my own mental suffering and give thanks. Jesus was extending His love to me through this nice nurse.

Philippians 4:6-7

"Do not be anxious about anything, but in everything, by prayer and petition, with thanksgiving, present your requests to God and the peace of God that surpasses all understanding shall guard your hearts and minds in Christ Jesus."

<u>Chapter 2</u>

Crash and burn. I've been there done that. I have been diagnosed with ADHD, Bipolar,

Schizoaffective, and Schizophrenic, but God knows I am able to bless others now.

I am so happy to be alive and my past is the silver lining.

Every diagnosis/problem list the devil has thrown at me has become an asset.

My History has become "His Story." Great redemptive journey because God is so good.

Been there done that. I have been suicidal, rebellious, riotous, you name it that has been me. Can God still use me? You bet!

<u>Chapter 3</u> – Journaling

I am going to have you read my journal if you would like.

I woke up this morning and didn't feel like coming into Justice in Mental Health Organization Drop-In. I felt lazy and unmotivated.

Yet, I knew it was important. I lugged a big bag of materials for art and now I'm here so glad.

Everyone is so nice to me—even those who have been my enemies.

What's the next step Jesus?

I know, facilitator group planning…

Ice Breaker:

If you could be anybody doing anything you want with your life what would you do and who would you be?

I would do exactly what I am doing. I am in my calling, but it hasn't always been this way—even recently.

God has opened the floodgates because He loves me.

Chapter 4 – Legalism

I am a hot mess. I mess up again and again, but God extends His grace 70 X 7.

I am just enjoying life, but it hasn't always been that way.

Before I was uptight, searching for a church that matched my doctrinal beliefs.

Now I say, "Just show Jesus!" Exemplify Him. Make a difference and reach out to the poor who cannot give back.

I am amazed when I see people contributing who expect no acknowledgment in return.

It's amazing and supernatural.

I have something to learn. The self-righteous have to show off their good deeds, but Christ followers don't tell anyone of their good deeds.

Praise be to God. I love the Body of Christ I belong to. We work together around the world to shine Jesus's love.

Love profound!

Love overwhelming!

Love that will drop everything to see that my or your soul is cared for.

This is the Body of Christ!

Woot...

We aren't big on doctrine, but mercy and forgiveness is our story and song. Hallelujah!

<u>Chapter 5</u> - My Cry

I want you to know I love you right now, just the way you are.

I don't know what kind of pain you may be going through, but our God is ever-present and cares.

He sent this book to you to bless you that you may see the light of God.

God is so real.

Take it slow. Slow down and appreciate the life God has given you just the way you were made.

You are special and have crucial shoes to fill!

The Body of Christ desires you on the team. Your make-up is crucial to reach the unreachable.

Why have we been through misery?

Well, it does build character, but also it teaches us to relate to those who no one understands.

You can save a life. You can walk in your calling. Pray on it today.

"Ask and ye shall receive. Seek and ye shall find. Knock and the door shall be open to you."

God blaze a way in the life of the person reading this book—in the name of Jesus, Amen!

You matter to me.

You matter to God.

Do not give up!

Pray and ask God what you are meant to do with your life. Ask Him and He alone will provide an answer.

Perhaps, you are meant to be inventive like me!

I created a Literary Free Zone at a mental health drop-in center. I am writing you from this venue right now.

I am having the time of my life with broken people like me.

I am sharing my friendship and story with anyone who wants to hear!

Give what you can in abundance to the needy—it's the Biblical way. "Pay it forward."

I like life because God blesses it. Thank you Jesus!

Flow in the Spirit by walking by faith. Be generous. Be loving. Be forgiving. Treat your enemies like royalty.

"All things are possible with God."

Chapter 6 –Downtime

I do not receive constant social stimulation nor should I. It is not healthy to be constantly busy.

We all need downtime to think, meditate and dwell with our Savior Jesus.

What do we do in these times?

I say have fun hanging with God. Do not make it a chore to dwell, meditate, and pray.

Talk to Him all the time!

Praise Him for He is good. If you do not have the attention span to swallow the whole Bible at this time, eat tasty morsels little by little.

Little by little adds up. Continual

investment in Jesus matters. Enjoy the

adventure!

<u>Chapter 7</u> – Blind Spots

No one is perfect, but God alone. We need each other. We all have aspects of our character that need refinement.

Since iron sharpens iron, lets bring it on!

Let's sup together. Let's fellowship and share our struggles. Let's get real with those we trust.

Hallelujah!

I love investing in people. It's my calling. God's children matter and extending mercy matters.

Give gifts to those who cannot pay back.

Open the floodgates; God bring the increase.

"The struggle is real."

Yes, everyone is going through something.

We must take the time to learn others' stories so we can properly love.

A listening ear means so much. Be an oasis in the desert to a person of need.

I love you and want you to have a great day. I want you to find more hope, peace, more joy!

Thanksgiving is crucial in this process. Be thankful at all times.

Find the silver lining and try to recognize something good in everyone!

Chapter 8 – Inclusion

The best projects allow and encourage everyone to participate. My calling in the Literary Free Zone does just this.

I love it when staff members come and relax to color. Praise the Lord! It is also so beautiful when people who do not normally connect find a point of connection!

Everyone has something to bring to the table. It is nice to not always be on duty. It is nice to relax and just be.

You matter and I love you. You have potential. You can make ripples in your calling today.

Pray for the Great Spirit to open

opportunities for you. Hallelujah!

Take it slow... How can I bless these people?

This is God's work!

"Do not judge a book by its cover." Do not search for someone who is the same as you. Pray about who you add to your circle.

We want to be a light to those in need—not just those who are similar to us.

Jesus said, "Whatsoever you unto the least of these, you do not me."

Look out for the interests of the needy. Be a friend to the friendless.

Chapter 10

Not every day is perfect or ideal. Some experiences can be disheartening and we can feel alone as leaders.

God makes a way and we are answerable to Him. I need Him right now. When positive vibes seem scarce, we must dig deeper. God help me with this self-declared facilitator for the Literary Free Zone.

Lord, prepare me for the Spring Conference. "Make a way oh God when there seems to be no way."

Chapter 11 – Counting Our Days

"You never know when your life might be demanded of you." "Tomorrow is not promised."

"Live life to the fullest."

Jesus is good and lived a breathtaking, productive life as our Lord and Savior on earth for 33 years.

He accomplished more than I could imagine in a shorter time than I lived.

"Live life to the fullest." "Shoot for your dreams." Never give up the faith!

Go all out! Give in secret to the miracle worker God Almighty!

He brings the increase.

Take time to reach out to everyone—

especially those of low position.

Care about those who no one cares about.

<u>Chapter 12</u>

Super Heroes are made just the way God made them. I am thankful for the opportunities God gives me.

Praise the Lord the sun is coming out too.

I give thanks for this day and for God giving me life. Life is a blessing to be shared.

I want to influence other lives for the better and follow the direction of our Lord!

Time spent investing in the rejects of society is not a waste, even when they have nothing to return.

I am so thankful God has given me a purpose to be a friend to the friendless!

Chapter 13

Today I wake up and ask myself, "How can I be a blessing to others while taking a Sabbath?"

Praise the Lord. He is in control and has other servants. We work together. Lord, prepare us to reach the masses. In the Name of Jesus, Amen.

Just be. Relax with God. Having a great day! I am thankful for those who serve and meet needs!

How does one relax and just be? It starts with thanksgiving and letting go of worry.

It involves making time with God a priority and considering Him in our daily lives.

Chapter 14

I am learning to rely on having little—depending on the provision of the Lord and helping others.

The Lord provides. He knows my heart to make a dent and making a dent requires all my commitment.

My poverty must seem foolishness to most. But I'm hardly entire. Sometimes I splurge on a pop or waste money on restaurant meals.

I live to depend on Jesus in this faith-walk. Show me the leaps and bounds. Help me to see through the storm in this life.

Let nothing distract the work of Christ in us.

Hallelujah! Great things are happening. The Lord is ever-present.

I am thankful for you and every word of encouragement from you. Some of you really build the Body. You are doing a great work.

Life can be hard many times and we need each other. Reach out to others. Be God's hands and feet.

Make a sacrifice for others.

<u>Chapter 15</u> – We Need Each Other

"Two has a better return than one; if one falls down, the other one picks him up."

I appreciate the practical ministry of my friend Michael. He gave of his heart to give me this nice laptop computer and did some of my dishes.

I don't even understand some of his gifting. He lives to serve the Lord in love.

To pour ourselves out like a drink offering in service and love.

I want to be all used up in this lifetime. I want to know that every bit of my life counts. I splurged on some food with my buddy and sometimes we do not see eye to eye, but I appreciate everyone working

together in the Body of Christ!

Chapter 16

These are the beginnings of end times when the Bible is banned from being seen.

I don't know where this situation is going, but Jesus is Lord and will be glorified.

Pray for me as I face this battle of heart for Freedom of Speech.

Things seem to be swaying in my favor. I did not expect this. I was told that if I didn't cover up the Bible, I would be banned for the day from JIMHO. I was told if I didn't follow the ban, the police would come.

<u>Chapter 17</u>

Oh give thanks and "anticipate great things." The Lord is my guide and He is in control.

I love my God and "With my God I can scale a wall."

Lead me on Lord to make wise choices. My weakness is pride. I cannot go about this life alone without some element of oversight.

"Pride cometh before the fall." And I follow you oh Lord. "Unless the Lord builds the house, the laborers build in vain."

Thank you Lord in all circumstances. Thank you Lord for abundance. "My soul shall delight itself as with the richest of foods."

Thank you Jesus for everything. Thank you for the fellowship.

Chapter 18

Unshakeable happiness... The Lord is building something special in all of us.

The Lord has a plan. "There are no accidents."

Get excited. Lets make a difference together!

Thank you God for giving people the heart to help!

Chapter 19 - New Season

Not everything goes our way every day. There are seasons of jubilee and seasons of testing.

I believe in everything Jesus is in control. I wait on the Lord and He renews my strength. I do not always understand the moment, but I place my trust and thanksgiving in Jesus.

I am still here. I still have a home. I still have a family. I wait on the Lord to have His miraculous way.

God is in control. He most certainly has our back!

When discouragement comes, we must not let our love grow cold, but rather press in...

When we tune into God, He begins to speak through us. Oh God help us day by day!

Chapter 20 – Rediscovering Satisfaction

What is the source of our joy? Is it resources or productive activities?

No one can put a finger down to push away the joy of the Lord. When everything is taken away, He is our strong tower.

I found great meaning in the Literary Free Zone for a time. Now, staff has eliminated this great source of meaning in my life.

I will not be crushed. I will stand for truth and give thanks in all circumstances.

As I wait for God's lead, I give thanks for nourishing food in my body and good friends.

I declare this a day of praise! How do I spend it oh Lord? What do you have for me in today? I want to be a blessing. I want to help people. I want to make a dent!

Under pressure, I write my heart. I want to change lives. I want to rescue the heart broken. I want to humbly show the love of God.

I am here alive, ready to worship. Nothing can snuff God's will for me. I am made for greatness and so are you. I am made to create a revolution of praise, meaning and love!

Sound the trumpet and exalt the name of the Lord. I am figuring this out. I am going out to meet the peoples. I am having a day of it. I am not giving up my choice to be joyful today!

This is a new day and I am going to give thanks. I will continue to remember all the great things God has provided for me. I have food. I have friends. Jesus is in my heart and He has led me to Plan B.

All Scripture used is taken from the New International Version and The King James Version of the Bible.

2nd Edition

Copyright Daniel Keith Arnold 2016,

Lansing Riverfront Press

Dedicated to the Passionate Believers I once opposed and to Jesus Christ who paid the ultimate price for truth.

OBEY GOD.

By

DANIEL K. ARNOLD

Obey God.

By Daniel K. Arnold

Testimony

I was distant. I did not know the requirements of my God and was wise in my own eyes. When I met the initial preachers, they seemed a turn-off, shouting that true repentance and change was necessary.

I created a piece of writing and made 150 copies to oppose them. One day, behind them God sent in reinforcements. A marine veteran shared his testimony and kindly invited me to Bible Study. He seemed noble and nice enough. When I went to the Bible Study I was horrified to hear the same message again. I stopped up my ears.

In my time of need, the door opened and I returned. One person planted a seed. One watered it, "but God made it grow."

You never know the complete results of your faithfulness to God! I told the man if he could possibly persuade me to the truth about repentance, I would tell the world.

In 2009, I wrote a long Facebook post about this message. In 2014, I converted it into the book, The Super Hero Manual II: Facilitating a Hideout Bible Study. In 2016, I finalized the book and as I read my words to edit, the Scripture had an effect on my heart again.

The Word does not return void. God's Word is living and active, real. My heart changed. Change can happen to anyone with "ears to hear." If you agree, pass this book on to your neighbor. Plant a seed. Let God make it grow

Obey God.

By Daniel K. Arnold

Chapter 1

"There is a way that seemeth right unto a man, but the end thereof *are* the ways of death (Proverbs 16:25, KJV)."

Popular Culture, Social Media, Life's Happenings. What seems right frequently is not right. Moral Truth is unchanging. There are absolutes. Whether someone calls himself/herself "heroic" or "ordinary," there exists an internal need to submit to a Higher Power.

Order involves submission. Order involves acknowledging that we are not God. In an age of moral relativism, where people redefine their own realities, who is there to turn to but God and His Holy Word?

The inspired Word of God can and will change lives.

In this new part of the year, written in January, almost everyone is aiming for a New Year's Resolution. People rarely shoot for the moon anymore though because they do not believe they can reach it. They have given up!

People have "tried faith" and it "didn't work."

The Bible says, "Ye lust, and have not: ye kill, and desire to have, and cannot obtain: ye fight and war, yet ye have not, because ye ask not. Ye ask, and receive not, because ye ask amiss, that ye may spend it in your pleasures (James 4:2-3, KJV)."

Rather than shoot for your own moon this year, point, aim, and shoot for what God asks you to aim for. Point to the will of God. Aim through His Word as you seek

Him in prayer and shoot for the moon by faith! God will help you bring His will for your life to pass. We must remain in the Vine of Christ.

"I am the vine, ye *are* the branches: He that abideth in me, and I in him, the same bringeth forth much fruit: for without me ye can do nothing (John 15:5, KJV)."

What does God require of us? There is a song from the Bible that explains:

"He has shown thee.

He has shown thee O Man,

What is good and what the Lord requires of
thee.

But to do justly,

But to do justly,

And to love mercy,
And to walk humbly with thy God.”

Webster's New Universal Dictionary

“Just” a. is defined as 1. Upright, honest,
having principles of rectitude, righteous, as
a just man.

Adv. Exactly, precisely

We should not live life by our own haphazard rules and morals. We need a Moral Code—the Bible—to live by. Our personal skewed definition of obedience misses the mark.

"For the wages of sin is death, but the gift of God is eternal life in Christ Jesus Our Lord (Romans 6:23)."

For "while we were yet sinners Christ died for us (Romans 5:8)." Now that we are restored to life, we must "continue in His kindness (Romans 11:22)."

We run the race with endurance.

Do you agree?

Or do you believe living for God is impossible?

Can we pick and choose how we are going to obey God's moral law?

This would be a conundrum; for there is forgiveness, but not license to sin.

"If we confess our sins, He is faithful and just to forgiveth our sins and to cleanse us from all unrighteousness (1 John 1:9)."

Who would take a bath and then throw select filth back on their body?

People are cleansed to be cleansed and to be as seen as blameless before Christ. Repenting is turning 180 degrees from our sin.

In the Book of Psalms, the Bible says, "As far as the east is from the west, so far has he removed our transgressions from us

(Psalm 103:12, NIV).”

Why would we return to our sins if they

only harm us?

“Whosoever committeth sin transgresseth

also the law: for sin is the transgression of

the law

(1 John 3:4, KJV).”

The Holy Spirit convicts us of sin found in

God’s Moral Law the Bible.

"But the Comforter, which is the Holy Ghost, whom the Father will send in my name, he shall teach you all things, and bring all things to your remembrance, whatsoever I have said unto you (John 14:26, KJV)."

Chapter 2

The Doctrine of Repentance

I grew up believing the popular consensus about sin. I was raised in church. I believed if I sincerely prayed a prayer of salvation, I would be Heaven bound, no questions asked.

When I was told otherwise, by some unpopular people, I at first all-out rebelled. I even spread literature against their message! Yet, over time, when I was thirsty for it, I was shown the truth at a Bible Study. I decided I would never come back when I heard what was being spoken, but God brought me back!

Over time, I would transition to believe the message I once abhorred.

I learned from this study, that God expects my best sacrifice, my best heart. I never realized it before.

On this adventure I went, breathing in and out the truths of Scripture until there was absorption.

Prepare to be shocked and prepare to let God speak to you as He did me:

But the question is, "Do I truly love them if I don't tell the complete truth?"

Am I worried that I may be rejected if I speak an unpopular message?

"Who the Son sets free is free indeed."

What does that mean to you?

Does it just mean you are free from worrying about your eternal destination? Is that all it means?

That one day you confess all your sins and turn to Jesus and the next day you are doing drugs?

People have various explanations for this...

[Opening]

1. Well, you can't judge them because the Bible says, "Do not judge or you to will be judged (Matthew 7:1)."

Look further...

1 Corinthians 5:12-13 (NIV)

"What business is it of mine to judge those outside the church? Are you not to judge those inside? God will judge those outside. "Expel the wicked man from among you."

It is quite obvious that if God tell us in the New Testament to expel someone from the Church who calls themselves a Christian yet is walking in sin that if they aren't even welcome in a church on this imperfect earth, that they potentially might not be welcome in a perfect world. Besides, they are considered "wicked" by God.

Ephesians 5:3-5 (NIV)

"But among you there must not be even a hint of sexual immorality, or of any kind of impurity, or of greed, because these are improper for God's holy people. Nor should there be obscenity, foolish talk or coarse joking, which are out of place, but rather thanksgiving. For of this you can be sure: No immoral, impure or greedy person—such a man is an idolater—has any inheritance in the kingdom of Christ and of God."

So I ask you, what is the definition of an immoral person? What is the definition of a greedy person? And why is that person an idolater?

Some may reason that the definition of an immoral person is based on how they believe Christ views them, regardless of their actions.

1 John 1:5-6 (NIV)

"This is the message we have heard from him and declare to you: God is light; in him there is no darkness at all. If we claim to have fellowship with him yet walk in the darkness, we lie and do not live by the truth.

Most people know that to walk in darkness is to commit any sin at all.

And here is where further human reasoning comes into play....

Let's go LOGICAL here for a second:

IF God is against divorce and Christ is married to us,

THEN, it's all good!

For better or for worse, right?

There was an exception:

Matthew 5:31-32 (NIV)

"It has been said, 'Anyone who divorces his wife must give her a certificate of divorce.'I tell you that anyone who divorces his wife, except for marital unfaithfulness, causes her to become an adulteress, and anyone who marries the divorced woman commits adultery."

In the Old Testament, God DIVORCED his people for being an "adulterous nation."

"I gave faithless Israel her certificate of divorce and sent her away because of all her adulteries. Yet I saw that her unfaithful sister Judah had no fear; she also went out and committed adultery (Jeremiah 3:8, NIV)."

Adultery against God in this way was to have a "lover" in addition to God-- aka idolatry.

As we read in the New Testament:

"For of this you can be sure: No immoral, impure or greedy person—such a man is an idolater—has any inheritance in the kingdom of Christ and of God (Ephesians 5:5, NIV)."

The Issue of Sacrifice

It is common knowledge that God expected His children to walk uprightly in the Old Testament.

But of course, everyone sinned from time to time.

If they ever sinned, they had to sacrifice a perfect lamb and repent.

Then, their sin would, as much as possible, be overlooked by God.

New Testament Sacrifice

Now, that Jesus has died on the cross and rose again, He is the perfect sacrifice that allows us to be one with the Father. However, we must still confess our sins whenever we commit them.

"If we claim to be without sin, we deceive ourselves and the truth is not in us. If we confess our sins, he is faithful and just and will forgive us our sins and purify us from all unrighteousness (1 John 1:8-9, NIV)."

We sing songs that God never changes, but do we really believe it?

Do we somehow believe that God expected His children to walk in righteousness in the Old Testament and now we are free through Jesus to live like the devil?

Remain in me, and I will remain in you. No branch can bear fruit by itself; it must remain in the vine. Neither can you bear fruit unless you remain in me. "I am the vine; you are the branches. If a man remains in me and I in him, he will bear much fruit; apart from me you can do nothing. If anyone does not remain in me, he is like a branch that is thrown away and withers; such branches are picked up, thrown into the fire and burned (John 15:4-6, NIV).”

How do we know we are remaining in Him?

Is it when the pastor tells us not to worry and assures us of our salvation?

“For God is not the author of confusion, but of peace, as in all churches of the saints (1 Corinthians 14:33, KJV).”

We don't need a pastor to do this. We need God. He is our final judge.

“But the righteousness that is by faith says: "Do not say in your heart, 'Who will ascend into heaven?'[" (that is, to bring Christ down) "or 'Who will descend into the deep?'" (that is, to bring Christ up from the dead) (Romans 10:6-7, NIV)."

There should be no question in the hearts of true believers as to their salvation.

However, it is possible to be deceived. It is possible to think you are hearing from God.

That is why the Bible says this:

 "Dear friends, do not believe every spirit, but test the spirits to see whether they are from God, because many false prophets have gone out into the world (1 John 4:1, NIV)."

"For the word of God is living and active and sharper than any two-edged sword, and piercing as far as the division of soul and spirit, of both joints and marrow, and able to judge the thoughts and intentions of the heart. And there is no creature hidden from His sight, but all things are open and laid bare to the eyes of Him with whom we must give account (Hebrews 4:12-13,NIV)."

The Bible has the final say. The truths inside are laid out plain as sight and the existence of God evident in nature so we are without excuse.

"All Scripture is God-breathed and is useful for teaching, rebuking, correcting and training in righteousness (2 Timothy 3:16, NIV)."

What do these verses mean?

"Since you have kept my command to endure patiently, I will also keep you from the hour of trial that is going to come upon the whole world to test those who live on the earth. I am coming soon. Hold on to what you have, so that no one will take your crown (Revelation 3:10-11, NIV)."

You mean I can lose my crown-- as in I had it before and now it's gone?

"Everyone will hate you because of me, but the one who stands firm to the end will be saved (Mark 13:13, NIV)."

Are you facing persecution for standing for the Truth or are you going with the flow?

If anyone has a question in his/her mind about how meaningful having anything between you and God is, consider this!

Now a man named Ananias, together with his wife Sapphira, also sold a piece of property. With his wife's full knowledge he kept back part of the money for himself, but brought the rest and put it at the apostles' feet. Then Peter said, "Ananias, how is it that Satan has so filled your heart that you have lied to the Holy Spirit and have kept for yourself some of the money you received for the land? Didn't it belong to you before it was sold? And after it was sold, wasn't the money at your disposal? What made you think of doing such a thing? You have not lied to men but to God."

When Ananias heard this, he fell down and died. And great fear seized all who heard what had happened. Then the young men came forward, wrapped up his body, and carried him out and buried him. About three hours later his wife came in, not knowing what had happened. 8Peter asked her, "Tell me, is this the price you and Ananias got for the land?"

"Yes," she said, "that is the price."

Peter said to her, "How could you agree to test the Spirit of the Lord? Look! The feet of the men who buried your husband are at the door, and they will carry you out also."

At that moment she fell down at his feet and died. Then the young men came in and, finding her dead, carried her out and buried her beside her husband. Great fear seized the whole church and all who heard about these events (Acts 5:1-11, NIV).”

These two believers sinned by lying. They had the opportunity to repent when Peter asked them what they had done. But they didn't and dropped dead in judgment for it.

What is sin?

“If anyone, then, knows the good they ought to do and doesn't do it, it is sin for them (James 4:17, NIV).”

Adam and Eve, before they ate from the Tree of the Knowledge of Good and Evil, could only commit one sin. No other sins had been invented yet.

If there is any area of sin that is not on your conscience, provided you haven't completely hardened your heart, it is my belief you are not responsible for it until you find out.

When you have done all this, be sure to guard against pride.

 "Pride goes before destruction, a haughty spirit before a fall (Proverbs 16:18, NIV)."

But if you should slip into pride for a second, do not fret, repent!

]

And last of all remember the whole entirety of 1 Corinthians 13.

To Summarize:

1.If I had all the spiritual gifts in the world, but have not love, I am nothing.

2.Love keeps no record of wrongs.

3.Love does not delight in evil, but rejoices with the truth. (So speak it even if it's unpopular!)

4.Love always hopes, always trusts, always perseveres!

Chapter 3:

Some One Sin Doctrine Reminders

Friend,

Here are some additional truths related to the "One Sin Doctrine" that I want to preserve.

1 John 1:9 (KJV)

"If we confess our sins, he is faithful and just and will forgive us our sins and purify us from all unrighteousness."

Jesus's Disciple John, addressed this verse to believers in his book, 1 John.

Even though they had committed to God initially, they still needed to continue to

confess their sins to God to be
continually be in a state of holiness and
blamelessness.

To confess means to literally profess with
your lips.

We confess out loud "Jesus is Lord" and
believe that He was raised from the dead
when we are saved.

We confess out loud, but only God needs to
hear it, any sin we have between us and
God.

I am sure you believe that God hears the
prayers of His children.

Consider this verse to consider who His
children are:"He that turneth away his ear

from hearing the law, even his prayer shall be abomination (Proverbs 28:9, KJV)."

"If ye love me, keep my commandments (John 14:15, KJV)."

For whoever does the will of my Father in heaven is my brother and sister and mother (Matthew 12:50, NIV)."

"By their fruit you will recognize them. Do people pick grapes from thornbushes, or figs from thistles? Likewise, every good tree bears good fruit, but a bad tree bears bad fruit. A good tree cannot bear bad fruit, and a bad tree cannot bear good fruit. Every tree that does not bear good fruit is cut down and thrown into the fire. Thus, by their fruit you will recognize them. "Not everyone who says to me, 'Lord, Lord,' will enter the kingdom of heaven, but only the one who does the will of my Father who is in heaven. Many will say to me on that day, 'Lord, Lord, did we not prophesy in your name and in your name drive out demons and in your name perform many miracles?' Then I will tell them plainly, 'I never knew you. Away from me, you evildoers (Matthew 7:16-20)!'"

My question to you is how much evil does one have to do to classify it as being evil?

"Enter through the narrow gate. For wide is the gate and broad is the road that leads to destruction, and many enter through it. But small is the gate and narrow the road that leads to life, and only a few find it (Matthew 7:13-14, NIV)."

"Be perfect, therefore, as your heavenly Father is perfect (Matthew 5:48, NIV)."

Is this a command or a suggestion?

If we are already perfect in God's eyes even when we sin and "don't have to confess it," why doesn't it say this instead?

"You don't have to try to be perfect, you already are."

But no, it says to be perfect-- as in submit yourself fully to God, confessing all the sins the Holy Spirit puts on your conscience through His voice or through the Word of God.

The first conclusion that we must come to is that the Bible is completely true and that "contradictions" are just parts of the Bible we don't understand yet.

"If we deliberately keep on sinning after we have received the knowledge of the truth, no sacrifice for sins is left, but only a fearful expectation of judgment and of raging fire that will consume the enemies of God (Hebrews 10:26-27)."

We all seem to have an interpretation of what it means to have faith and experience God's grace.

A true man of faith has enough faith coupled with Holy Spirit's power to completely surrender himself. Pretty much we all did this when we were initially saved. We gave up all idolatry between us and God--- any stronghold of sin.

Sure the next day we broke God's moral law again in some areas, but we need to confess those areas. And each day we improve. Grace is unconditional forgiveness that requires us bringing our sin before God. It isn't the freedom to sin and hold onto our sin.

1 John 1:5-10 (NIV)

"But if we walk in the light, as he is in the light, we have fellowship with one another, and the blood of Jesus, his Son, purifies us from all sin. If we claim to be without sin, we deceive ourselves and the truth is not in us. If we confess our sins, he is faithful and just and will forgive us our sins and purify us from all unrighteousness. If we claim we have not sinned, we make him out to be a liar and his word has no place in our lives."

1. No one is without sin. All must first realize this.

2. However, if we confess our sins then we are purified against all unrighteousness.

3. Then, we are right before God.

In terms of salvation by faith, not by works, this is true.

It is faith that saves us, nothing we can do. For no mere man has walked in perfection his whole life and even the one sin he has committed along the way has separated him from God. It is faith and one who has faith that Jesus is Lord of his life, is in complete surrenderence to Him. He doesn't let any sin remain in his life that the Holy Spirit reveals.

However, at the same time, "faith without works is dead." Now just how much action do we need to take in obeying God? One good deed?

"But Samuel replied:"Does the LORD delight in burnt offerings and sacrifices as much as in obeying the voice of the LORD ? To obey is better than sacrifice, And to heed is better than the fat of rams (1 Samuel 15:22, NIV)."

"If you love me, keep my commands (John 14:15, NIV)."

And when we don't obey, we need to get right with God.

"What shall we say then? Shall we continue in sin, that grace may abound? God forbid. How shall we, that are dead to sin, live any longer therein (Romans 6:1-2, KJV)?"

"For if ye live after the flesh, ye shall die: but if ye through the Spirit DO mortify the deeds of the body, ye shall live (Romans 8:13, KJV)."

And in terms of grace, here's a definition you may not be familiar with:

GRACE

3. Favorable influence of God; divine influence or the influence of the spirit, in renewing the heart and restraining from sin.

My grace is sufficient for thee... 2 Cor.12

Definition from Webster's American Dictionary of the English Language, 1828.

This is far from the license to sin, but rather a soul saved by "grace" is under the influence of the Holy Spirit and thus is restrained from sin...

Under this influence, the soul can't stand to have any sin between him and God.

The following verses from one of Jesus' parables, explains falling away.

"This is the meaning of the parable: The seed is the word of God. Those along the path are the ones who hear, and then the devil comes and takes away the word from their hearts, so that they may not believe and be saved. Those on the rock are the ones who receive the word with joy when they hear it, but they have no root. They believe for a while, but in the time of testing they fall away. The seed that fell among thorns stands for those who hear, but as they go on their way they are choked by life's worries, riches and pleasures, and they do not mature. But the seed on good soil stands for those with a noble and good heart, who hear the word, retain it, and by persevering produce a crop (Luke 8:11- 15, NIV)."

Let that crop produce in you. And share the truth you know with others.

Conclusion

Life is a time of constant discovery. Do not be surprised if you learn new things each day or even discover that what you once thought to be a lie is truth. Search out a matter for yourself until you are thoroughly convinced in your own mind.

Ask God to minister to you personally and let His truths liberate you!

God Bless,

Daniel K. Arnold

Talk To God

By Daniel K. Arnold

Dedicated to Marissa Poullion who took the time to listen as I poured out my heart with an exhaustive Gospel message and to God who makes our lives beautiful.

Talk To God

By Daniel K. Arnold

God will guide you. Give Him a chance. It is with tremendous difficulty that I begin this important book. I need God's guidance to write.

Communing and talking with God is everything to a Holy Spirit filled believer. It is not a matter to be taken lightly. This matter can confuse the outside world, but to the true believer God's voice is a great comfort.

I do not know where to begin when talking about tuning into the voice of God.

Jesus is my everything. He is the source. His life as our Savior is everything. Nothing would be possible without Jesus.

Spirit guides can try, but Jesus sent the True Comforter—the Holy Spirit. Jesus spoke:

"But the Comforter, which is the Holy Ghost, whom the Father will send in my name; he will teach you all things and bring all things to your remembrance—whatsoever I have spoken unto you." (John 14:26)

That's right: "All things." There is no lack to what the Spirit of the Living God can teach us.

How does God speak? One may wonder.
The experience may vary from person to
person.

My Medical Record:

R/T AUDITORY HALLUCINATIONS. PT
REPORTS "SPEAKING TO GOD AND GOD
SPEAKS TO ME." 10/30/18 1730 TPRN.

I do not hear audibly from God, but a
doctor interpreted my statement that I talk
to God this way. My style of
communication with God is through writing.
I write to God and God writes back to me
through comforting thoughts He puts in my
head.

This the world cannot understand. At the
same time, this guidance means everything

to me. Every day of freedom is a blessing. People do not understand my joy, but God is my source. God talks to me. He blesses me every day. Life is a gift and now you are part of my story.

Every reader matters and needs hope. God's hope does not disappoint. Jesus speaks to me directly. It's such a blessing. He can do the same for you. Before Jesus left this earth, He said He would send the Comforter—the Holy Spirit.

In the Book of Acts of the Bible, the believers waited together in the Upper Room for the Holy Spirit to fall on them.

All believers can experience the power of the Holy Spirit in their lives. He is no respecter of persons.

"For God so loved the world that he gave his one and only son that whosoever believes in him shall not perish but have eternal life." (John 3:16)

The first step is belief in the saving power of Jesus who died on the cross, was resurrected, and gave us the promise of the Holy Spirit. Shortly after the Holy Spirit fell on Pentecost. Peter gave a directive to all believers:

"The Peter said unto them, Repent, and be baptized every one of you in the name of Jesus Christ for the remission of sins, and ye

shall receive the gift of the Holy Ghost."
(Acts 2:38)

Do you know how liberating it is to submit to the call of God and be led by the Holy Spirit? God wants to speak to us and clearly.

"There is therefore now no condemnation to them which are in Christ Jesus, who walk not after the flesh, but after the Spirit." (Romans 8:1)

The Spirit of the Living God is essential in our lives.

"For to be carnally minded is death; but to be spiritually minded is life and peace."

(Romans 8:6)

This is my opus. This book is very important to me. I want you to learn how to communicate clearly with God in a way that the world cannot shake. A man truly liberated cannot be shaken. You can lock him up. You can put him in a hospital and shoot him up with drugs. You can kill him like they crucified my Lord and claimed he had demons.

But anywhere you send a True Believer, they will prosper. Everywhere you send him or her becomes part of the mission. Apostle Paul is noted as writing, "To live is Christ, to die is gain." (Philippians 1:21)

Super Heroes have faced it all and their joy cannot be taken away. They live lives of purpose and do not back down for anyone. Super Heroes answer to God first and foremost. You do not have to understand their journey, but they know their Savior.

If you kill him or her, Heaven is the next experience for him or her.

In the Book of Acts, God launched the first believers. There were no accidents. They knew what they were about and were unbreakable. Yes they were misunderstood—even when unified. When the Holy Spirit fell on them in the Upper Room, some thought they were full of new wine. The supernatural is impossible to understand with natural fleshy eyes.

The way of the Spirit is for those whose eyes have been opened.

"For the preaching of the cross is to them that perish foolishness; but unto us which are saved it is the power of God.

For it is written, I will destroy the wisdom of the wise, and will bring to nothing the understanding of the prudent.

Where is the wise? Where is the scribe? Where is the disputer of this world? hath not God made foolish the wisdom of this world?" (1 Corinthians 1:18-20)

"But God hath chosen the foolish things of the world to confound the wise; and God hath chosen the weak things of the world to confound the things which are mighty.

And base things of the world, and things which are despised, hath God chosen, yea, and things which are not, to bring to nought things that are.

That no flesh should glory in his presence. But of him which are ye in Christ Jesus, who of God is made unto us wisdom, and righteousness, and sanctification, and redemption. That according as it is written, He that glorieth, let him glory in the Lord." (1 Corinthians 1:27-30)

Follow the Living God. Give your life to Christ and be blessed forevermore. Stephen lived a glorious life to the end. He laid out a beautiful sermon when challenged to the death. His saga ended beautifully and continued on into eternity.

"When they heard these things, they were cut to the heart, and they gnashed on him with their teeth. But he, being fully of the Holy Spirit, looked up stedfastly into heaven, and saw the glory of the Lord, and Jesus standing on the right hand of God.

And said, Behold, I see the heavens opened, and the Son of Man standing on the right hand of God. Then they cried out with a loud voice, and stopped their ears, and ran up on him with one accord. And cast him out of the city, and stoned him; and the witnesses laid down their clothes at a young man's feet, whose name was Saul.

And they stoned Stephen, calling up on God; and saying, Lord Jesus, receive my spirit. And he kneeled down, and cried with a loud voice, Lord lay not this sin to their charge. And when he said this, he fell asleep." (Acts 7:54-60)

The Light shines beautifully through early church believers, but guess what? The saga is not over! We can follow the Spirit today. We can be empowered today. It comes at a cost, but it is worth it. God tells us to take up our cross daily. It was Jesus's teaching before He led by example by actually dying on a cross. We may have to pay the ultimate price to follow Jesus, but it is fully worth it. God deserves our full commitment. Do not be afraid. Press forward. Run the race for Jesus.

"He who endures to the end shall be saved." (Matthew 24:13)

God makes it possible for us to live a glorious life following His promise. I love my life. You can too.

Let God lead you and talk to you. Let Him whisper words of comfort and meet you on your individual journey. We all have a unique experience with God. Some see visions. Some dream dreams. Some operate in miracles. Some have the opportunity to see mountains move. "With man it is impossible, but with God all things are possible." (Matthew 19:26)

Don't ever give up. You are not an accident.
God has created you for a beautiful reason.
Look for the silver lining. There is hope in
the worst of circumstances if we turn our
sorrows over to Jesus. Do not ever end
your life. God has a beautiful plan for you.
You matter.

"Give Jesus a chance." Beautiful things
happen at our breaking point. "And he said
unto me, My grace is sufficient for thee: for
my strength is made perfect in weakness."
(2 Corinthians 12:9)

Give God your mess and let Him paint a
masterpiece. God loves you. He sees
potential in you. He wants to give you a
purpose. Give Him a chance today.

"Seek Him while he may be found. Call on him while he is near." (Isaiah 55:6)

"Ho everyone that thirsteth, come ye to the waters, he that hath no money; come ye, buy and eat; yea, come buy wine and milk without money and without price." (Isaiah 55:1)

This is the day of salvation for you. Come to the Lord now. If you heart is not ready now, what will compel you to be liberated? Come to Jesus while your heart is open. He loves you so much. The past is over. There is forgiveness of sins.

"Com now, and let us reason together, saith the Lord; though your sins be as scarlet, they shall be as white as snow; though they

be red like crimson, they shall be as wool."
(Isaiah 1:18)

"If we confess our sins, he is faithful and just to forgiveth our sins and to cleanse us from all unrighteousness." (1 John 1:9)

Start over today. Give your heart to Jesus and let your heart be made glad! Our adventures have just begun. It doesn't end there.

"Therefore do not worry about tomorrow, for tomorrow will worry about itself. Each day has enough trouble of its own."
(Matthew 6:34)

God has our back. There is nothing too hard for God. Expect great adventures. Never give up. Press on. Love at all times. Give God your all!

It is so worth it. He will not disappoint. Put your trust in Jesus today. Listen to His voice in your life. Be inspired. Tell the world.

"Behold, I stand at the door and knock; if anyone hears My voice, and open the door, I will come in to him, and will sup with him, and he with me." (Revelation 3:20)

These are Jesus's words to encourage those that seek the Lord. He will answer!

God is organic. He will teach us new things if we simply open up our eyes and hearts. He has our best interest at heart. Go on. Talk to Him. Tell Him exactly what is on your mind. He cares. He died for our well-being because we are worth it to Him.

Jesus provides a solution to all worries. The Word says, "Do not be anxious about anything, but in everything, by prayer and petition—present your requests to God. And the peace of God that surpasses all understanding shall guard your hearts and minds in Christ Jesus." (Philippians 4:6-7)

Let Jesus guide you today and forever. Write down your thoughts to God and let Him respond. Tell Him what's on your mind. Work out your stream of consciousness. Continue to read the Bible to gain more revelation and clarity.

Do what you love and share it with Jesus. My little sister Kristin likes to sing and dance. She has special moments of worship before the Lord. My brother Jason likes to hike in nature.

We all have unique ways of communicating with an infinitely intricate God. Find your love language and share what you love with Jesus.

The rest is just adventure. Oh the times of bliss knowing that the God of this universe wants to communicate with us. Eternity allows for this experience to last forever. We will never be abandoned.

Thanks,

Daniel